Neymar

A Biography of the Brazilian Superstar

BENJAMIN SOUTHERLAND

Visit Benjamin Southerland's website at
benjaminsoutherland.com.

ISBN: 1534760520
ISBN-13: 978-1534760523

Table of Contents

Chapter 1: A Born Legacy

Neymar da Silva Santos was playing professional football for Uniao Mogi das Cruzes Futebol Club when his prodigy son was born. He began his soccer career with the Santos Juniors team. When he was sixteen, he began to play professionally with Portuguesa Santista. He made many moves during his short professional career, flitting from one team to another. His father, Pai, has admitted that he was not a stellar player, but some of his teammates disagree. They have proclaimed that he was "good with the ball at his feet. An old-fashioned forward who did not score many goals but was good at playmaking and crossing the ball." He played well enough that, in 1989, he was able to negotiate a new contract with the help of investors and earn enough to buy his parents a house in São Vicente and a nice car for himself.

At the height of his career in 1991, he married his teenage sweetheart, Nadine Gonçalves. They were eager to start a family and welcomed a son on February 5, 1992. The da Silva Santos family lived in a middle-class neighborhood outside the town center in an average-sized apartment paid for by Club Uniao. Neighbors remember them as a quiet family who didn't attract attention.

In June 1992, the family was driving from Mogi das Cruzes to visit Pai's parents on the coast in São Vicente. Pai had just played an awesome league match against Matonese, during which he had scored the game-tying goal. They were traveling a dangerous mountain road, during a rainstorm, which made conditions even more treacherous. Four-month-old Neymar Jr. was strapped in a crib in the backseat and Nadine was in the front passenger's seat. Pai panicked when he saw a car coming head-on on his side of the road. He tried to swerve out of the way, but avoiding impact was impossible. The other car hit them broadside on the driver's side and almost sent them careening off the side of the mountain. Their car was suspended on the side of the road, so they could not escape through the doors.

Pai's legs were crushed and he could not move, but his only thoughts were of his son in the backseat. Neither he nor Nadine could see or hear the baby. They thought he had been thrown from the car. Nadine was able to climb out the back window and flag down help. Once rescuers arrived, they were astounded to find the baby Neymar Jr. under rubble in the back floor board still alive. He escaped the accident with only a cut on his forehead. His father, however, would spend almost a year in the hospital, at a rehabilitation facility, and on rest at home trying to regain full use of his legs.

Neymar Pai did not give up easily. After extensive rehabilitation, he continued to try to play soccer, but he would never play at the same level of greatness as before. In 1996, the family welcomed a new baby girl, Rafaela. With a growing family and financial concerns, Pai made the decision to move his family to São Vicente to live with his parents in the house he had bought for them. His plan was to secure a new contract to play soccer while also working in his father's garage. He did play for a while for Batel de Parana and Varzea Grande, but the constant travel was taking a toll on his body and his family, and the contracts were becoming less lucrative. So, in 1997, Pai knew his dream of a profitable career in soccer was over and he had to focus on providing for his family.

Chapter 2: A Child Prodigy

The family struggled financially during Neymar's early years. Pai worked three jobs attempting to support his family and help his parents. He worked in his father's garage as a mechanic while also working as a salesperson and delivery driver. Nadine worked as a cook in a local child-care center. Still, it was hard at that time to earn a decent living in Brazil. Pai recalls it as a time when "We weren't starting at zero—we were starting at minus-five." He recalls the times there was no money for electricity and the family would gather their resources and make the best of their circumstances. He remembers that Neymar Jr. and Rafaella actually liked sitting in candlelight. In his biography, he stated, "What we had in that house with no electricity was priceless: true love. That's how you really build a home, a life. With love. Even without money, our family was united and happy."

Nadine has described Neymar beginning to show his passion and talent for soccer when he was just a toddler. He would chase after balls at any risk, and instead of the typical stuffed animal, he slept with a soccer ball. She recalls that, at one time, he had as many as 54 soccer balls in his bed. Pai remembers being amazed that even at three years old, Neymar would play ball with his feet instead of his hands. In the cramped house the family shared with his grandparents, Neymar would contrive drills in the narrow ways between furniture and walls. He used his sister and cousins as defenders and goalkeepers. He played with the older boys in the streets using whatever they could find to use as a ball. He has stated, "They were very dismissive, the other boys. 'Who is this little kid?' But I managed to convince them to let me play that first time, and I scored a goal. That changed their attitude. That changed everything." He was only four or five, but he was building the skills and agility which would one day captivate the world.

But, it wasn't his skill with the ball that first got noticed. He was playing and running in the stands at one of his father's games when his first coach, Roberto Antonio dos Santos (Betinho) spotted him and noticed his athleticism and agility. Neymar was skinny—wiry—and Betinho noted uncommon coordination and effortless running for such a young boy. The coach recalled in an interview, "I asked a friend, 'Who is that boy?' I looked at the father:

he was well built and had good ball control. I looked at the mother, who was attending the match: she was tall and thin. I immediately began to think about the genetics of Neymar Jr.'s parents: they were two fine biological specimens. This made me wonder how the little one would play football." Betinho was coaching Club de Regatas Tumiaru and was putting together a team of players born in 1991 and 1992 for the São Vicente league. He asked Pai and Nadine to let Neymar try out. They agreed and Betinho was amazed at the little boy's talent. He stated, "He was different to the others; you could have put him with 200 kids his age and he would have stood out just the same."

Like most Brazilian soccer greats, Neymar's career began on the futsal court. Futsal is a Brazilian-style indoor game played on a basketball court with a small, heavy soccer ball. The space is tighter than a pitch and players must have excellent ball control and agility. It is a faster-paced game, so quick reflexes and creative dribbling are a must. Players need masterful use of both feet to dribble, pass, and shoot. They need to think ahead of play and be able to dart in and out while maintaining control of the ball in limited space. This practice at futsal created the freestyle handling of the ball that Neymar has mastered.

Neymar played futsal for a year under Betinho at Tumiaru. Over the next few years, he followed his coach to Portuguesa Santista and Gremetal. In interviews, Betinho has said he knew he had found a great talent because "Neymar was different: he was a very intelligent player. He was always one step ahead. He was the first to arrive at training and the last to leave the pitch. I cast my mind to Robinho at the same age and Neymar seemed more talented." With each move, he told Pai to trust him saying, "You have a son who can be one of the greatest footballers. He will be at least as good as Robinho."

Neymar and Rafaella had been attending the inadequate public schools in São Vicente. When he was nine years old and Betinho had negotiated a place for him at Portuguesa Santista, his coach and Pai also negotiated a scholarship for him and Rafaella to a prestigious private school. Pai and Nadine were very concerned about their children's opportunities and wanted the best education possible for them. Pai has said that he wanted Neymar to have a good education to count on in case his soccer career did not come to fruition. His classmates and teachers described Neymar as fun-loving and happy. He was a good student who worked hard. He earned average marks and was always very respectable to his teachers and coaches. The coordinator of the school, Maria Antonia, said, "He was always ready to play with his classmates. At break time, students were not allowed to play football but he always found a way around it. He would go to the head-master and beg him to lend him a football so he could take some shots or practice kick ups."

The school was looking to improve its own football program, so Neymar's scholarship would secure him as a star for their team. He was playing for his school team and for Portuguesa. Elton Luiz, a manager at Esportes Futsal, at the time noted, "He was in a league of his own both on and off the pitch. He just loved playing with the ball. Training was three times a week but he showed no sign of it bothering him." His youth coaches all describe him as smart and happy during those years. He was a good friend to his teammates and they admired him. Although he often stole the show in matches, there was never any jealousy or animosity. He was a humble kid and enjoyed being part of the group. Alcides Magri, Junior, one of his youth coaches says, "When he was on the pitch, he changed. He was able to turn a match around on his own. But, he was not a showoff on the pitch."

Although Pai's work caused him to miss most of Neymar's matches, he knew the media was proclaiming his son a soccer sensation. Local papers were publishing photos and articles about the young prodigy from Praia Grande. In 2005, Neymar's training and school schedule were so rigorous that he had little time to devote to the school team. His school teammates started to complain that he was receiving special treatment and shouldn't be allowed to miss practices and still play in matches. His school coach, Mateus Pavao Fuschini told Neymar he had to attend school training. Neymar did and consistently outplayed his teammates. The school won the TV Tribuna Cup that year, and it brought a lot of attention to the skinny kid who was being called a magician with the ball.

In 2003, news about this young soccer wonder reached Jose Ely de Miranda (Zito), who was the coordinator of the junior teams at Santos Futebol Club at that time. He had heard so much praise about Neymar that he went to a Portuguesa Santista match just to watch him. He recalled in an interview, "Neymar filled me with joy. He was only eleven years old, but he did the same things then as he does today. With the ball at his feet, he was incredible, sensational. He was miles about the rest. A real superstar." He knew that Santos had to get a commitment from Neymar immediately before another club lured him away. What resulted was Neymar's first contract. It was for five years with a salary of 450 reais a month. He had received some compensation and bonuses from clubs before, but this monthly salary allowed Pai to quit working so many hours in order to become Neymar's full-time manager and agent. Nadine was able to quit work and be more available for the children as well.

Pai was also able to negotiate a place for Neymar's old coach, Betinho, at Santos. Pai knew that it was important

Neymar be supported by people who would care for his best interest. He was even able to convince Santos to include a fuel allowance for Betinho so he would be able to help transport Neymar to school and practices. Betinho has said he owed his job with Santos to Pai's skillful negotiating. When Neymar arrived at Santos, another coach became an important role model in his life: Antonio Lima dos Santos (Lima).

Santos had no eleven-a-side team for the under-13s, so Neymar had to continue training and playing at futsal under Zito. Lima kept hearing about his amazing talents and convinced Pai and Zito to allow him to play soccer with the fifteen-year-old team. Neymar was only twelve and Zito was afraid he was not strong enough physically to play in that higher age division. Lima convinced them that Neymar could begin with just training and not move directly into league play. Many of the clubs were notorious for playing players older than the age limit. It was not Neymar's skill that worried Zito. It was his skinny build which would make him a target for intimidation.

Lima remembers Neymar as very obedient and easygoing for his age. He was willing to try any training regimen his coaches suggested and he was very determined to be successful in every match. He was always up for a challenge and willing to give his best in every situation. Lima remembers, "When I explained to him what I wanted from him from a training session, you could be sure that Neymar would always achieve what you were trying to achieve." Lima says the only challenge Neymar ever shied from was using his left foot. He is naturally right-footed, so even though he could, he was not as confident shooting and passing with the left. Today Neymar's ambidextrous play amazes opponents, teammates, and fans.

Chapter 3: Taking on the World

Neymar's talent at Santos was gaining global attention when he was only twelve to thirteen years old. His former teammate, Leo Baptistao, remembers, "What he does now on the pitch, he was already doing at the age of ten, eleven. Let's just say that the tactics for lots of matches were just to pass the ball to Neymar and let him get on with it." Yet, they all remember that he remained humble and always exuded love and excitement for the game. His coach, Lima, has often said it was Pai's influence which contributed most to Neymar's work ethic and respectable attitude. Neymar has often been quoted praising his father: "I'm extremely lucky that I have more than a father; I have by my side, more than anything else, my best friend. He is sometimes harsh with me, but everything he does, he does for me, for us. For our family."

Clubs from all over were courting the young star and making great efforts to lure him their way. When he was 13, Real Madrid made a very lucrative offer to try to convince Neymar to make a move. The trip was his first plane ride, his first time being away from home for an extended period. They hosted him for three weeks and were amazed by his abilities during tryouts. Coach Jesus Gutierrez stated, "He was a lot better than the other players at that stage. These weren't your average footballers." The offer would require Neymar to move to Spain and grow up through Real Madrid. It would be a guaranteed future with an extraordinary paycheck for a young boy. But, ultimately Neymar and his father decided to gamble on Santos's ability to make him a superstar soccer player.

Pai accompanied Neymar to Spain, and he reported that his son grew homesick early in the trip. He felt the experience was too overwhelming for the boy, who had not often been away from home and who grew up sharing a bedroom with his siblings. Pai later said, "On these occasions, you have to trust your paternal instinct. I've had many struggles in my life. I'm an adult, a grown man, but my son was still just a kid and I could sense that he felt overwhelmed by it all." Pai has said that Neymar was playing well, but he grew sadder each day and was completely out of his comfort zone. They decided together that he needed to grow up playing in Brazil. It was too early for him to make such a move, even if they would be turning down a large sum of money. Pai also stated, "All I wanted was for him to continue to play with joy. And there was no joy for him in Madrid in those days, and no money could ever change that."

Neymar wanted to stay with Santos, so a new contract was negotiated. At 13, he was already a very successful player and the club was willing to invest in his future. They, too, offered a handsome amount for the family to stay in Brazil. With 10,000 reais a month, the family was able to move into a better, larger apartment closer to the club, and Neymar and Rafaella would receive renewed scholarships at a prestigious private school. Neymar was receiving a lot of attention and was under tremendous pressure to live up to the expectations which accompanied being such a celebrated player. He has stated the pressure to prove himself worthy of all the hype was sometimes intense.

By the time he was fifteen years old, Neymar was appearing for Santos in the Under-18 Copa São Paulo, Brazil's premier youth soccer competition. Although he was the youngest player, he was becoming a star and continuing to enjoy global recognition. Lima had Neymar on a special diet and weight training program in order help him become more muscular and more physically competitive in the older division. He was becoming more comfortable using his left foot, and teams around the world had their eye on him. Santos would soon attach a $25 million release clause to his contract with a salary which was also becoming significantly more lucrative.

Lino Martins, who coached Neymar from age sixteen to seventeen, described him as smart, charming, and sensible. Lino says he worked with Neymar at a very "critical age, an age when you can see whether a kid is going to make it, if he will become professional." Most players with that much talent will lose their way, but Lino credits Pai for understanding the risks and advising his son well to be humble and disciplined. Neymar understood that even though he possessed great talent, he still had a lot to learn and needed an excellent work ethic to continue advancing.

His 2009 performance in the Copa São Paulo was so stellar that talks began immediately afterwards to move him on to the first team. He was already training with the juniors, but Marcio Fernandez, the coach, wanted to move slowly. Neymar was fitting in, even with the older players, but his physical abilities were still worrisome. He still needed a bulkier physique to compete against older, more muscular players and more experience for a more physical level of play. Fernandez commented, "I put him in the reserve first team so that he could get experience and see what professional life was like. There was still time before moving to the first team. The fans must be patient." On February 12, 2009, Neymar was allowed to travel with the first team to a match against Marilia in a Paulista league match. Fernandez did not let him play, and Santos lost 1–0. Fernandez later commented, "I thought he was going to play in the match. I did not play him and I regret that." The team had not won a major match in over nine months, and Fernandez was forced to resign shortly after this match.

In December 2009, Vágner Mancini took over as manager and helped Santos secure their first major win for the season. They beat São Paulo 1–0. It was the first time they had beaten São Paulo in the Campeonato Paulista since 2000. During the match, the 24,000 fans packed in the stadium began to chant Neymar's name to convince Mancini to play him. Neymar came on fifteen minutes into the second half and the crowd loved it. Luca Caioli recalls, "There had never been anything like it in the history of Santos FC. Or at least, no one can remember a player who received as many standing ovations even before he got on the pitch, the euphoric chanting for the seventeen-year-old to be sent on." Neymar missed his shot by hitting the post that night, but he has said it still felt like a victory since the team won and he had so much fun enjoying the crowd and atmosphere.

On March 15, 2009 in Pacaembu Stadium in a match against Mogi Mirim, Neymar's objective was to score his first goal for Santos. He planned for it to be the first of many. In the 27th minute of the second half, he realized his chance. The ball was passed infield toward the goal. Neymar happened to be free and launched a diving header and fired the ball into the net. Santos won the match 3–0. Neymar's grandfather, Seu Ilzemar, had recently passed away, and Neymar recalled how much his grandfather and father had loved Pele's famous fist pump, so he did it after the goal in honor of them both. The crowd was going crazy, and the television commentator was declaring, "The kid from Santos shines! This is an historic goal right here! This is an historic date for Brazilian football." Neymar himself has stated it's his sheer love and excitement for the game which inspire his elaborate celebration moves. In his father's biography, he stated, "I'm still the same guy who once watched the matches from the stands or on TV. Except that now I'm on the pitch and I can score for the team. When I do, I'm so happy that I can't help but celebrate like crazy."

Neymar went on to finish the season with 14 goals in 48 games, and was awarded the league's Best Young Player award. Santos, however, suffered some important losses which caused Mancini to be released. He was replaced by Vanderlei Luxemburo who had coached Santos during several seasons in the past. After a couple of matches, Neymar was benched. When Luxemburo was questioned, he stated, "He is little and cannot withstand the physical contact of a match. He looks like Robinho when he started. He needs to build up his muscle mass. I do not want to burn him out." Vanderlei also commented that Neymar looked like a "stick insect", a nickname which stuck. Neymar was again prescribed a high-calorie diet and intensive weight training. This meant that the star player who had just signed an 80,000-reais-a-month contract with a 90 million reais leave clause was almost always sitting the bench.

By December 2009, Luxemburo had again resigned. He was replaced by Dorival Junior who believed he had a group of young players which Santos had trained well and who could be trusted. Neymar would have his chance to shine again. Santos was expected to have a stellar team in 2010 with Neymar, Robinho, Ganso, and André. They were expected to bring the club's first trophy in six years, they would deliver big with the Paulista state championship and the Copa do Brasil at the beginning of the season, with Neymar scoring 25 goals in two competitions, earning him the award Best Player of the State Championship. The pressure was on Brazil's manager, Dunga, to call Neymar up for the 2010 World Cup, but for whatever reasons he did not. Neymar did get his debut for Brazil in August 2010 in a match against the USA that Brazil won 2–0.

During an afternoon before a match in August 2010, Neymar and his teammate Andre were playing around the way teenage boys might and decided to do something fun with their hair. They came out for the match sporting Mohawks and the fans loved it. Neymar Sr. stated he was not so happy and suppressed his urge to wring Neymar's neck on the pitch. They would later have a conversation about reckless and impulsive behavior, but Neymar scored two goals in that match. So, he was allowed to keep the Mohawk for a while, and Neymar Sr. began to enjoy its popularity in Brazilian culture. Everyone started sporting the hairstyle in honor of their favorite player. Neymar Sr. once stated, "In Brazil, only the president doesn't have a Mohawk."

Another phenomenon that swept Brazil because of Neymar's great success at Santos was termed "Neymarization". Children, and some adults, began to believe if they focused solely on soccer, they might be able to propel their careers to the level of Neymar. People were quitting their jobs and ignoring other responsibilities in an effort to foster their football talents—or lack thereof. Edu Marangon, a former coach at Paulista, commented in an interview that people were forgetting that "a Neymar is born every 50 years." The phenomenon was born partly by the sheer exuberance Neymar was bringing to the game. Marangon went on to say, "For a time, Neymar single-handedly transformed Santos into the Cirque du Soleil (the show that children and adults alike want to see at all costs). He is the new

Messi. It is, however, a shame that he has given birth to 'Neymarization'" Adding fuel to the Neymar craze, Pelé made a comment in an interview that was widely publicized and that he later may have regretted. He flippantly commented that Neymar might be even better than he was.

It did appear that Neymar was having the time of his life. He described his exuberance as, "I just like playing with the ball," he said. "I always have. I play on the street even now. When we're on vacation—it doesn't matter where—I will go and look for a game." His joy for the game influenced and spread to his teammates in 2010. Working and celebrating together they transformed Santos football. Caioli stated, "It was the spreading of joy and desire to have fun which oozed from the pores of the latest generation of *Meninos de la Vila*." Neymar scored an astounding 42 goals in 60 games that season, and fans continued to look forward to catching the latest celebration dance. "They invented one dance after another: the baseball hat and rap, the tennis match, the motorbike, the lorry, the rolling planes, the merry-go-round, the military march, the shoe-shiner, and the signature dances to music from movies. The range of dances seemed endless." Neymar has stated several times that it was indeed the best year of his life.

The Santos 2010 team lived up to their hype and produced Santos's best season in years. They won both the Paulista state championship and the Copa do Brasil. Neymar was named Best Player of the State Championship and finished as top-scorer of the Copa do Brasil. In December, he was named to the Brazilian championship Team of the Year. However, issues did begin to surface during this glorious season which made some wonder whether Neymar's antics were going too far. He was often criticized for diving and exaggerating in an effort to be awarded fouls and penalty kicks. Some would say his dramatics were bordering on cheating. In September, Dorival gave the penalty kick for a foul on Neymar to another player. Neymar argued to the point where he had to be calmed down by a teammate. Dorival wanted Neymar suspended for his behavior, but the club sided with Neymar, and Dorival was soon released. Neymar apologized for his attitude and the incident, but the media and his critics were taking note of his unflattering behavior.

After the incident, Neymar faced a barrage of criticism in the press. He was called "a monster", "a bad boy", and "an out-of-control rebel". As part of his apology, he stated, "It was the worst day of my life. I cried all day. I came home completely gutted to see my father and mother crying too." His parents were at the stadium and were reportedly appalled by their son's behavior. The club received bad publicity for its decision to side with an eighteen-year-old worth 80 million reais over a successful coach who had just won two titles. Journalist, Paulo Vinicius Coelho, summed up what many were thinking by writing, "Neymar is now the king of the castle at Vila Belmiro, which is exactly what an eighteen-year-old kid should not be allowed to think."

Clubs around the world, however, were not deterred by his antics. In 2010, interests and offers poured in. Two which were most notable and highly publicized came from West Ham and Chelsea. West Ham offered £15 million, which sounded appealing until a few days later when Chelsea offered £22 million. Santos refused to accept less than £30 million, and reports were that proved too much for Chelsea, and Neymar decided against moving to Europe. Santos reported they were not interested in selling their star, and Neymar Sr. said he still felt it was too soon in his son's career for him to make the move to Europe. Neymar commented to the press that he was honored by the offer and would someday love to play in Europe.

Neymar was heralded by the media and fans as a patriotic hero for turning down the European offers, but Santos's increased offer must have played a large part in his decision. They had enlisted sponsors to raise the funds to offer an exorbitant amount for a teenage player. It was a five-year contract with a leave clause of £45 million and a salary of 600,000 reais a month. Second only to Ronaldo, he became the highest-paid player in Brazil.

Negotiations included speeches about patriotism and the clincher might have been a personal call from the king himself, Pelé. Neymar commented, "Even Pelé called me. Can you imagine how important I felt? The King of Football called and asked me to stay. He reminded me of his entire career with Santos, his five world titles with the national team and the club, and all the recognition he received. It wasn't easy but it was the right decision for us. We did the right thing for our family, friends, and my career."

Santos was rewarded for Neymar's high price tag in 2011 when he led the club to its first Copa Libertadores championship in 48 years. He scored six goals in the competition, tying him for third top goal scorer. Santos also won its second state, and for the second time, Neymar was named as the best player of the competition. He fulfilled a life-long dream of playing in the Copa America, even though Santos was disappointed by a second-round loss to Paraguay. Neymar went on to finish the season with 14 goals in 17 matches, and was awarded the very prestigious South American Player of the Year award. Santos was disappointed again in the finals of the Club World Cup in Japan with a loss to Barcelona. Neymar, however, was awarded the coveted Bronze Ball awarded mostly for his performance in the victory over Kashiwa Reysol. And, adding to the list of extraordinary accomplishments was the impressive 2011 FIFA Puskás Award for his goal against Flamengo, in a 5–4 loss.

Neymar was set in 2012 to surpass his former accomplishments and enjoy even greater success on the pitch. On February 5, his 20th birthday, the country of Brazil celebrated with him as he scored his 100th goal against Palmeiras in the Campeonato Paulista. Santos was the 2012 Campeonato Paulista champions. Neymar finished with 20 goals and was voted the Best player and Best Forward, and was joint top scorer in the Copa Libertadores with eight goals. Santos, however, could not hold on to their title and were beaten by Corinthians in the semi-finals. Neymar's other many awards during the season included the Golden Ball, the Arthur Friedenreich Award, and the Armando Nogueira Trophy. In addition, he retained his award as the Best South American Footballer of the Year.

A sour note in the season came with the 2012 Summer Olympic Games. Brazil has never won Gold, but this seemed like the year it would happen. The Brazilian team seemed more than stacked with exceptional players who looked good in the early stages. Neymar scored three goals and assisted on several to lead Brazil into the finals against Mexico. Mexico was considered the underdog, but they pulled off the 2–1 win against Brazil for the Gold. Neymar and his teammates faced harsh criticism for their less-than-stellar play in the final match. They were clearly dejected on the platform receiving the Silver.

Rumors were at their height at the end of the 2012 season that Neymar was ready to move to Europe. The offers and enticements from clubs all over the world were pouring in and it seemed highly unlikely that they would continue to be ignored. His contract with Brazil, running through the end of 2014, was negotiated to keep him in the country until the 2014 World Cup. It would be difficult to think money was an issue as his salary and sponsorships with Brazil were staggering. So, in late 2012, he continued to give the same answers to the allegations that he was entertaining offers from other clubs: "I have the dream of playing in Europe but I feel the right moment hasn't come," he told UOL. "I am happy at Santos, close to my family and friends. When the right moment comes, I will leave. But I don't feel like playing in Europe now. I am not afraid. I am just happy at Santos." It was obvious that Real Madrid and Barcelona were the top contenders to lure him to Europe, and many who had followed his career thus far speculated that the move would happen when his agent and his father decided the time and offer were optimal.

The announcement came on Sunday, May 26, 2013. Neymar first posted on social media: "I am not going to wait until Monday. My family and friends now know my decision. On Monday, I will sign with Barcelona." His contractual terms were complicated and costly. He would have to be bought not only from Santos but from investors as well. The contract, which was reportedly agreed to, paid Santos and the investors around €28m, plus another €30m to the player and an estimated €9m in agents' fees. Neymar signed a five-year contract for a salary of €7m a season. His total package is worth more than €100m. Neymar commented, "Money is OK but happiness takes priority. We decided to come to Barcelona. I had a lot of offers, but I followed my heart. I think adjusting to European football may be difficult, but I hope to adjust quickly."

Before leaving for Barcelona, Neymar tried to prove his Brazilian patriotism in July by leading Brazil to victory in the 2013 Confederations Cup. In his last game with Santos on May 26, he reportedly sobbed during the national anthem before the match. In his few years with Santos, he led the club to their best seasons since Brazil legend Pelé. He remains the club's leading scorer after Pelé with 138 goals in 229 matches. His hope was that he was ready for the next level of European football at Barcelona. He hoped his humble spirit and work ethic would bring the same success he had enjoyed at home. In an interview, he commented, "To have the opportunity to play with great players I admire like Messi, Xavi, and Andres Iniesta—I've begun a new stage of my life and I'm going to be very happy and achieve a lot."

Chapter 4: The Deadly Trio

Neymar had been warned that his success at Barcelona might depend upon his relationship with Lionel Messi. More prestigious players than he had been released due to their inability to mesh with Barcelona's star. Rumors abounded that Messi himself was always entertaining offers from other clubs, and he wasn't keen on what he had heard about the exorbitant contract which had won Neymar. Many believed, however, that if these two prodigies could gel as teammates, they could be a deadly combination for Barcelona.

Neymar made his competitive debut for Barcelona during the opening game of the 2013–14 La Liga season in a 7–0 win against Levante UD. He scored his first goal for Barcelona on August 21st in the first leg of the 2013 Supercopa de España against Atlético Madrid. On December 11, Neymar scored his first three Champions League goals in a hat-trick in a 6–1 win over Celtic in

Barcelona's final Group H match. He finished the season with 39 goals in all competitions and 10 in the Champions League. He shared the highest scorer rank with Cristiano Ronaldo and his teammate, Lionel Messi. However, with Messi out injured for large portions of the season, Barcelona did not fare as well. There were no trophies for the club, and their costly stars were under criticism.

In 2015, things started to turn around for Club Barcelona. When Messi returned, what club officials had hoped for came together. Rather than creating jealousy and animosity among teammates, Messi and Neymar gelled as leaders, and along with Luis Suárez, they formed what became an unstoppable triad. The threesome ended the 2015 season with an incredible 125 goals, making them the highest scoring attacking threesome in Spanish football history. The world was truly impressed by the lack of individualism each showed and their commitment to working together for the good of the team. Many believe they will continue to make the best front line the sport has ever seen. Of the collective 175 goals Barcelona scored in 2015, only 53 were not contributed by the amazing trident of Messi, Neymar, and Suarez. In a recent interview with Fylan and Armand, Neymar shared his thoughts on being a part of the famous trio: "They are two superstars and we get along very well on and off the pitch. So everything comes together to make it work. Even though we have a very strong rivalry on the national teams—Brazil, Argentina and Uruguay—we get along really well. I'm really proud to be part of this trident and proud that we are making soccer history. We don't want to stop now, we want to keep writing history."

Neymar's first season at Barcelona might have ended trophy-less, but the second season more than made up. Barcelona became the first club in history to win the treble of Liga, Copa del Rey, and Champions League twice. Even though he was out sick with the mumps for two weeks, Neymar came back to take his La Liga goal total to 14 goals in 12 games. For the season, he had more than 40 goals. When he scored the final goal in the match for Barcelona to beat Juventus 3–1 and complete the historic treble, he also became the eighth player in history to win both the Copa Libertadores and the UEFA Champions League. And, even better, he became the first player ever to score in final victories for both competitions. In an interview after the match, an emotional Neymar stated, "Now I think there is nothing left to claim, there is nothing more you can say about me." A few months later he would be recognized for his many efforts in Barcelona's successful season as he came in third behind Messi and Cristiano Ronaldo for the highest football award and honor of the year, the 2015 FIFA Ballon d'Or.

Chapter 5: International Play

Although it was widely believed that Neymar would play for Brazil in the 2010 World Cup, Coach Dunga never called him up on the team. Pelé and Romário both reportedly urged Dunga to put Neymar on the squad and a petition with more than 14,000 signatures was filed, but Dunga stated that while the eighteen-year-old was incredibly talented, he did not have enough experience in international play to earn a spot on the Brazilian home team. By July 2010, Dunga had been replaced by Mano Menezes who did call Neymar to play on August 10th in a friendly match against the United States. Neymar scored his first goal for the Brazil senior team in the 28th minute of that match. He would go on to play in the 2011 Copa América in Argentina where Brazil was eliminated in the quarter-finals.

He was selected for the Brazilian Olympic Football Team for the 2012 Olympic Games in London. He scored his first Olympic goal on July 26th against Egypt in a 3–2 victory for Brazil. He would assist Brazil in making it to the finals to play for the gold where they lost to Mexico 2–1. He scored his first international hat trick on September 10, 2012 in an 8–0 win against China. In 2013, he played in the Confederations Cup where he scored the first goal of the tournament in a 3–0 win over Japan. Brazil won the tournament in a final 3–0 victory over Spain, and Neymar received the Golden Ball award for best player of the tournament.

On March 5, 2014, Neymar scored a hat-trick in a friendly against South Africa in Johannesburg, but the hat-trick was overshadowed in the press by his attention to a little boy who ran onto the pitch at the end of the match. Security was about to usher to little boy off when Neymar scooped him up and carried him to meet his Brazilian teammates. They lifted the little boy in the air during their celebration and then took pictures with him. The video and pictures went viral on media the next day, and the public couldn't help but gush over Neymar for his generosity toward the adorable little fan.

Hopes were high in Brazil in 2014. With the star, Neymar, Brazil expected to win its sixth World Cup. Then, in the quarter-final match against Colombia, Neymar took a knee in the back by defender Juan Zuniga. He suffered a fractured vertebra in his spine and was not able to finish the tournament. Brazil beat Colombia 2–1, but lost to Germany in the semi-finals. Even though he couldn't play in the semi-finals, Neymar was awarded the Bronze Boot as the third top goal scorer for the tournament. The Brazilian national team and its coaches faced scathing criticism from the press and public for falling apart after Neymar's departure from the tournament. The 7–0 loss to Germany was called a massacre, and the third place playoff match against the Netherlands ended in a disappointing and humiliating 3–0 loss.

Coach Dunga was dismissed after Brazil's disappointing performance at the 2010 World Cup. But he was hired back in 2015, and this time, he was putting his faith in Brazil's superstar, Neymar. With former captain Thiago Silva out due to injury, Dunga named Neymar the new captain of the Brazil national team. Dunga told ESPN, "He is a reference point for Brazilian football. He has great quality and, despite his age, he is experienced. The captain is an example for all of his teammates overall. We have to have a strong group so that Neymar can grow more each day, as a player, as a person, being an example to children."

In Brazil's second match in the 2015 Copa America, which resulted in a 0–1 loss to Colombia, Neymar was booked for an alleged handball which led to what was called "melee" on the pitch after the final whistle. He was red-carded for purposely kicking the ball at Pablo

Armero's head and attempting to head-butt Jeison Murillo, the only goal scorer of the match. He was then cited for angrily confronting and verbally abusing referee Enrique Osses in the tunnel leading to the dressing room. CONMEBOL, South America's governing body for soccer, issued Neymar a four game suspension in addition to a $10,000 fine. Neymar commented to the press, "In my view, the rules are always used against me. I was off-balance, the ball hit my hand, but it was not intentional. They put a weak referee in there to whistle up for all that. The team didn't play well." Colombian striker Carlos Bacca, who pushed Neymar in the altercation, was also red-carded, but Neymar felt he had been targeted throughout the tense match. The Brazilian football federation (CBF) did accuse referee Enrique Osses of being hostile toward Neymar during and after the match.

The question in 2016 is whether Neymar will be called up to play in the Copa America for its 100t anniversary, or he will play in Rio in the 2016 Summer Olympic Games, or he can physically take on both. He definitely has something to prove at both. Brazil was embarrassed after he was forced out of the Copa America in 2015 and would certainly like to make a comeback to restore its dignity in that important tournament. But they were embarrassed in the 2012 Olympic Games as well after Neymar suffered a fractured vertebra and couldn't continue to carry his home team to the gold. Most analysts believe that if it is at all possible, Neymar will try to compete in both competitions. However, Olympic teams can only play three over-age players and Neymar would fill one of those spots if chosen. Rio will host the 2016 Olympic Games, so taking Gold in his home country would certainly seem a priority. Jones quoted Brazil's national team coordinator Gilmar Rinaldi as saying, "We are going to talk with the players and the clubs. It's a physical question. In the coming days, Dunga will give me names of the three over-age players he proposes for the Olympics. After the qualifiers in March against Uruguay and Paraguay, we will talk personally with those players."

Neymar told Fylan and Armand, "They said that in the World Cup it wasn't gonna work, but everything worked out well. I believe it will work well in the Olympics also and I expect to be able to represent my country really well and bring the expected gold medal that we never won in soccer."

Chapter 6: Controversy

To be subjected to public scrutiny and held in the spotlight at such an early age can surely take its toll on young athletes and celebrities. Neymar was subjected early on to the stress which comes with stardom as a teenager when many fold to the pressures of new wealth and celebrity status. Yet, he seemed to stay above scandal, devoting his life to soccer and school only. His father worked to surround him with people who would help take care of his image and work ethic as well as his soccer career. Stories have surfaced that he has been spotted at parties or nightclubs, perhaps partying a bit too much, but, as he told CNN in 2012, "I'm 20 years old, I have to take advantage of being young." He seems to have maintained a fairly clean image for someone who had it all at such an early age. He and those near him give most of the credit to his father who they say kept him humble and focused. Neymar also told CNN, "It's hard, especially for me. I want to do this and that, but I have to follow a line. I'm a professional player and a professional athlete. I have to resist some things to get ahead in the future. That's my life."

The first thing that did not go unnoticed in the press and public eye was his becoming a father out of wedlock at age nineteen. The scrutiny, speculation, and rumors were brutal for Neymar and the baby's mother, Carolina Noguiera Dantas, who was only seventeen. She reported that she experienced so much harsh publicity she went off social media and tried to live very privately for several years. Eduardo Musa, one of the 14 members of Neymar's team of advisers, said: "It was overwhelming, and what we did not want people to forget was that it was not a money issue or anything else. It was a baby. That was the important thing."

Neymar reported that he was very scared about the responsibility and very sorry for embarrassing his family, and he intended to take his responsibilities as a father very seriously. He commented, "Everything in my life has happened very early, personally and professionally. I'm always learning. I have to."

The baby, David Lucca Silva Santos, was born on August 24, 2011. Neymar and Carolina have remained close friends and are committed to co-parenting. The baby lives with his mother full-time, and Neymar supports her with a £8,000 per month support agreement and she now lives in a five-bedroom penthouse in Santos bought by him. She was quoted by Shahin praising Neymar as a father: "Juninho is a marvelous, caring, doting father and a friend who has stood by me. When he was at Santos, he would come as often as he could, he was caring and showered him with gifts. Sometimes he stayed the night to sleep with David." Little Davi is often seen at Neymar's matches and in photos with the star player doting over him as Neymar reportedly makes every effort to send as much time as possible with his son. He has stated in several interviews that whatever ugliness preceded Davi's birth has been overshadowed by the joy he feels as a father.

Another major controversy for the Santos family began in January 2014 when suspicions were raised that Barcelona had not been honest about the financial terms of Neymar's transfer from Santos in 2013. Barcelona reported that they paid a total of £48.6 million for the young star, but club member Jordi Cases suspected the price tag was much higher. Reportedly, the club was beginning to suffer some financial strains and Cases wanted answers to questions about where some funds had been appropriated. When club officials wouldn't answer his questions, he turned the issue over to Spanish courts who opened an investigation into the club's misappropriation of funds and possible tax fraud. The club's president, Sandro Rosell, who had handled Neymar's transfer negotiations, soon resigned under intense speculation. The new president, Josep Maria Bartomeu, opened the records and revealed that the transfer had actually cost Barcelona £71.5 million. Most shocking in the list of actual fees paid by Barcelona was a £33 million unreported compensation fee paid to Neymar's parents.

Barcelona hoped that by disclosing their records and paying £11 million to the Spanish treasury as a "complimentary tax declaration" they would satisfy authorities and close the investigation. However, it seemed to make investigators more determined to study the controversy surrounding the terms of Neymar's transfer. Club president, Bartomeu, claimed the issue was really related to the disagreements over who is responsible for some of the tax on the various agreements and contracts. He stated, "It's embarrassing because we think we are right. We are not happy with the situation but we will defend our club very strongly when the judge will call us to declare." The Barcelona club president, Bartomeu, and former president, Rosell, were charged with tax fraud and prosecutors have asked for jail time of up to seven years for Rosell, who was also charged with misappropriation of funds. In addition, the club, Bartomeu, and Rosell would all be responsible for millions in unpaid taxes. The case is still in trial.

As Neymar's acting agent and manager, Neymar Sr. was, of course, at the center of the controversy. He was berated in the press for negotiating such an unethical and greedy deal on his son's behalf. Neymar came quickly to his father's defense saying, "I am sick and tired of this... I've had enough of all this talk. I am a fan of my dad for having put me where I am, and if he makes millions from that, what's the big deal? He worked for it; it didn't just fall in his lap." However, others had much more to say about Neymar Sr.'s part in the transfer case. In February 2016, the São Paulo federal court froze more than £32 million worth of assets owned by Neymar and his family. Neymar and his father are being accused and are under investigation by Brazilian tax authorities for tax fraud in excess of £11 million for possibly concealing earnings through their network of three companies.

The tax fraud investigation was spurred by the court case brought by the Brazilian investment fund DIS, which owned 40 percent of Neymar's image rights while he was at Santos. DIS claims it was cheated out of its rightful share in the dishonest transfer deal with Barcelona. Delcir Sonda, the Brazilian owner of DIS, was one of the investors who sponsored the very young Neymar to keep him from transferring to Chelsea in 2010. He told Badcock, "I feel betrayed personally and economically. This was a trick between Barça, Santos, Neymar, and his father." He also advised Neymar from a Madrid press conference, "You are a fantastic player and I don't want you to go down in history for your criminal acts. You must show your strength on and off the pitch and I hope you can resolve your judicial problems in Brazil and in Spain."

Santos officials have issued scathing statements and allegations about Neymar Sr. since the investigations began over a year ago. They claim that part of Neymar Sr.'s incentive to transfer his son included an orgy with prostitutes in London arranged by Barcelona. They too claim they were cheated out of millions in the infamous deal. A representative of Santos told the Spanish court investigating the case that Santos had sent an appeal to FIFA's arbitration panel about suspected concealed extra fees of which the club should have received a 60-percent share. All of the controversy surrounding the shady transfer is currently in trial or under further investigation. The many constituents involved may wait years for judgments about who should pay for the many misappropriations.

Chapter 7: Personal Life

In 2012 and 2013, *Sportspro* magazine named Neymar the most marketable athlete in the world. That status has earned him more than $17 million a year in sponsorships and endorsements. Some of these high-dollar endorsement deals have been with Nike, Panasonic, Red Bull, and Volkswagen, to name a few. He is also known for promoting the Brazilian modern pop music called Música sertaneja. A video of him dancing in the Santos locker room in front of teammates to Michel Teló's hit "Ai se eu te pego!" went viral on the internet receiving millions of hits in just a few days. He appeared with Teló in one of his concerts. He had a cameo appearance in the music video of the hit sertanejo song called "Eu Quero Tchu, Eu Quero Tcha" by João Lucas & Marcelo in 2012. He then appeared on a rap music video called "País do Futebol" by MC Guimê in 2013. He also starred in the 2014 Beats by Dre World Cup advertisement called "The

Game Before the Game". He teamed up with other famous footballers for the short film which showcased famous players' pre-game rituals.

Neymar also enjoys the status of the fourth highest social media rank among athletes in the world. Like Cristiano Ronaldo, Neymar has appeared on the covers of *Pro Evolution Soccer 2013* and *Pro Evolution Soccer 2012.* The Brazilian magazine Placar's front cover caused a stir in 2012 by featuring Neymar crucified on the cross with the caption "The Brazilian ace turns scapegoat in a sport where everyone plays dirty." In April 2013, Brazilian cartoonist Mauricio de Sousa released a Monica's Gang comic book with a young Neymar as the main character. In February 2014, he became the first Brazilian athlete ever featured on the cover of *Time* magazine.

Neymar has used part of his fortune to fund the Neymar Junior Project Institute. The institute, which opened in December 2014, includes a football field, swimming pool, and classrooms for up to 2,500 students age 7–14 in Neymar's childhood home, Praia Grande, São Paulo. In an area where drugs, prostitution, and juvenile delinquency are high, the institute aims to give children a safe place to not only play, but to also get help with academics. The institute will eventually offer medical and dental services for its students as well. FC Barcelona has partnered with the Neymar Junior Project Institute to promote sports as a means of social integration for children in South American countries.

In 2014, Neymar, PayPal, and Waves of Water teamed up and used the World Cup as a stage for their project to bring clean water to Brazil. Fans could make donations through PayPal to the fund which provided clean water filters to impoverished areas of Brazil. Neymar also released autographed memorabilia to be auctioned on eBay. All sales went to Waves of Water to purchase the $50 filters which provide up to a million gallons of fresh water. Jon Rose, founder of Waves for Water, stated, "Neymar is passionate about this. We have done multiple partnerships and projects together, and he understands the importance of who he is."

Chapter 8: Conclusion

With the cloud of legal proceedings hovering nearby, Neymar's image is a complex one. His critics describe him as a greedy exhibitionist and a spoiled child. His supporters claim he is humble and fun-loving with an altruistic spirit. One thing for sure is the young star is nearing Pelé's goal scoring record, and there are few who would argue that he won't make history and far surpass it. When questioned about future plans, Neymar says, "Football is a child's game grown-ups take seriously. But it doesn't need to be serious all the time. I want to have fun. I want to make people happy. I want to keep playing, dribbling and scoring. If a child has a dream, he must chase it. And never give up, even if people say it will never come true. I want to be the boy who never stopped dreaming."

About the Author

Benjamin Southerland is a lifelong Chicagoland resident. Southerland developed a strong interest for politics and government during his college years through his study of leaders who have shaped history, such as Winston Churchill, Napoleon, and Thomas Jefferson. Southerland is also interested in individuals who have impacted the world of sports and entertainment. He has studied and written about politicians, world leaders, athletes, and celebrities. He researches these fascinating figures extensively in order to determine what has shaped their worldviews and contributed to their success. He aims for his books to give readers a deep understanding of the achievements, inspirations, and goals of the world's most influential individuals. Follow Benjamin Southerland at his website benjaminsoutherland.com to learn about his latest books.

Made in the USA
Middletown, DE
13 December 2022

18426321R00029